DATE DUE

THE ULTIMATE GUIDE TO
WINDSURFING

NIK BAKER & DAIDA RUANO MORENO

THE ULTIMATE GUIDE TO
WINDSURFING

NIK BAKER & DAIDA RUANO MORENO

THE LYONS PRESS

First Lyons Press edition, 2001

First published in the UK 2001
by CollinsWillow
an imprint of HarperCollins*Publishers*
London

Copyright © 2001 by HarperCollins*Publishers*

This book was created by Chilli for HarperCollins*Publishers* Ltd.

1 3 5 7 9 8 6 4 2

ISBN 1-58574-305-4

Color reproduction by Saxon Group

Printed and bound in Italy by Rotolito, Lombarda

The Library of Congress Cataloging-in-Publication Data is available on file.

Edited by: Craig Jarvis & Rob Bryant. Design by: Chilli/Dakini Ltd.
Photography: Chilli/John Carter, Alex Williams and Cutre/Daniel Miquel

With thanks to: Ben Marcus — *Surfer* Magazine

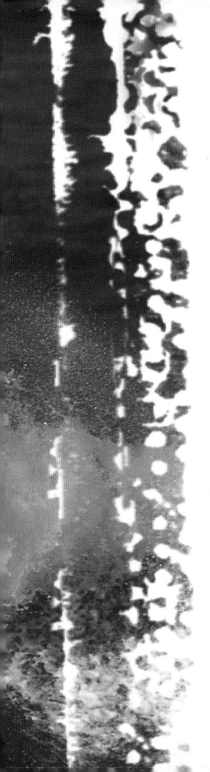

contents

" **windsurfing is** life, freedom, fun, action, pleasure, entertainment... **windsurfing is everything** "

"The first time I went out, the first time I put my feet on the board, even the first time I picked up the sail, it was absolutely incredible! I felt like I was flying.
An incredible feeling went through my body and I wanted to keep going faster and faster all the way to the horizon.
The problem arose when I wanted to come back in.... but I started to sail with my sister and a few other friends who helped me to swim back to the beach with the equipment.... I think it is really important to start windsurfing with other people, so you can help each other." **– Daida**

"Windsurfing hasn't just been a part of my life, but it has been my entire life for 17 years now, and I have this feeling it will remain so for at least that amount of time again. I need it like I need to eat. The first time I even saw a windsurfer I was 12 years old and we were on a family holiday on an island in Tunisia called Kirkena. My dad and I rented a board and splashed around for hours until I managed to get going for about 100 feet. I remember the feeling of being so free. It was amazing to be flying along on the water at such speed that I literally could not sleep at night for wanting to get up in the morning just to have another go and get back that feeling." – **Nik**

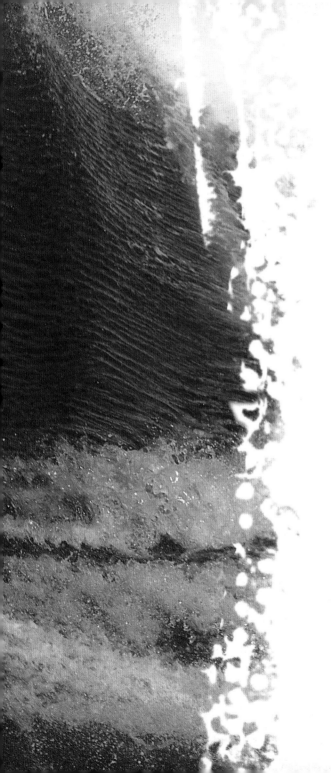

1
windsurfing
– a way of life

Why must I be a teenager in love? Windsurfing gets into your blood and in your soul. At first it is just traipsing around on your holidays with a hired rig and taking the kids for little jaunts in mild winds across smooth water. Soon it starts becoming a little more in-depth, and you find yourself wanting to experience all the excitement it has to offer. Then, before you know it, you're hooked and it's crazy. Like a lovestruck teenager you start displaying strange personality quirks and irrational behaviour. Maybe you start wearing strange clothing, talking in an unusual dialect only known by people with similar clothing and even changing your hairstyle as you fall under the spell. It has the power to take over your life and control your every mood and emotion, and thus your life. Life is all about fun, and the fundamental need for a human being to have fun is irresistible.

Left: Pozo, Gran Canaria — My home beach during a PWA contest. Now where did I leave that sail? — Daida

Opposite: There's always time to relax at the beach.

You find yourself keeping a constant, almost subconscious watch on the weather. Staring out of the window from the office and watching the wind do its work amongst the highest branches and low clouds. You might even find yourself viewing a stretch of windswept water and mindsailing across it with a new rig. Or working out what the conditions would be like at your favourite spot miles away. Before you know it you are bailing on commitments, rescheduling your tasks, reprioritising and making excuses to go windsurfing. Pushing your personal limits. Dreaming of flying, of birds in the sky. It's so much like being in love – except you're awash with adrenaline. The thrill of the hunt, unknown and unexpected variables, the peril of foreign danger. The dread of getting uncontrollably in debt as your need for more and more equipment escalates with your improving skills.

To experience riding on the shoulder of a giant Jaws wave in Hawaii, to fly high through the air off the back of a massive, wind-swept wave. Even just to visit a beautiful, coral-fringed and tranquil tropical island in pursuit of windsurfing highs, it is usually an experience that is life changing. How many equatorial sunsets are you actually going to witness in one brief lifetime? How many people who are actually trapped in wearisome, internet-based, credit-card, high-rise lifestyles actually ever get to see dolphins and whales in their natural habitat? Some windsurfers retire from standard sports; some leave their girlfriends, their home towns and even their careers to seek out opportunities and relationships that are more advantageously suited to chasing this profoundly powerful experience with nature. How many people actually follow their dreams? It's a simple addiction.

To windsurf is to be healthy, tanned and robust. To constantly have your hair made thick from crusted salt and sand. To be driving home after a day at the beach, sunburned and tired and sore from a day's sailing amongst giant, windswept waves, eyelids caked with salt crystals, and to be happy in the knowledge that you know something that the rest of the world is quietly oblivious to.

Most people go down to the beach on those startlingly calm days – when flags hang listlessly in tepid air and the sun is blazing down and burning all in the grasp of its deadly rays. When the car parks are filled by ten o'clock in the morning, and the sand is just a myriad of different coloured towels, different hued people, and bright parasols. When the heat makes it absolutely necessary to spend long hours in the cooling seawater.
These are the days for the beach.

Not when it's blowing a gale and stinging sand is smacking hard against bare skin. When white horses are huge, arcing sheets of crazy, wind-swept spray. This is the best time for a windsurfer, but not for the poor girlfriend. Still, loads of downtime on the beach, on tropical islands and beautiful peninsulas make it all worth it.

Travel

"It's such an amazing feeling to be sailing in some of the best windsurfing locations in the world; then to be able to just quickly pack my stuff, jump on to a plane, and in a few hours be sailing in another unreal windsurfing location with another bunch of enthusiastic windsurfers. I've had the opportunity to sail and visit some truly beautiful and some not so beautiful locations in the world. From Germany, France, Turkey, Portugal, England, Italy, Spain, Ireland, Scotland, over to America, Mexico, Hawaii, Brazil, South Africa, Australia, New Zealand, New Caledonia, Fiji and more. What other life would give these experiences of so many cultures and people around the globe?" **– Nik**

"Oh! The travel thing. Planes, planes and more planes. I think this is the worst part of being a professional windsurfer. To travel so much. Especially if you have to take planes all the way from Gran Canaria to Maui, it takes me at least 33 hours to get there, that is if I don't spend any overnights in any airports... But the destination always makes the hardships of travel worthwhile. You can use all the time available in the planes to read a bit and work out your mind. Once you have your boom in your hands and head out for your first sail you soon forget about all the discomforts of getting there..."
– Daida

Above Right: When the conditions are right you just want to sail until dark.

Opposite: When they arrive the waves at Jaws on Maui's north shore provide the sail of a lifetime for any windsurfer.

Above: Esperance, Western Australia where the powerful waves of the Southern Ocean meet the beautiful Antipodean coast.

Opposite Top: The north shore of Maui is a windsurfing paradise.

Opposite Below: The Fijian island of Namotu – 360º of wave sailing heaven.

There are so many locations out there and so many experiences to be had that it is so hard for us to pick any out. To name a few:

Rocking all over the world
Australia – With its strong surf culture and ninety percent of the population living on or near the coast, Australia also rates as one of the world's top windsurfing destinations. From the strong breaks on the southern shores of Victoria and Esperance in Western Australia to the raw power of Margaret River in the south-west, and the long flat stretches along the windy west coast. It comes as little surprise that so many of the world's top competitors come from the land down under.

Fiji – Capturing the spectacular power of the Pacific Ocean, Fiji is perfectly placed to deliver some of the most challenging and enticing waves on the planet. For the adventure-driven wave sailor, Fiji is a place of joy and wonder, and despite the unreal sailing, a place of rare beauty. A trip to Fiji for whatever reason will most definitely result in a return.

USA – Despite the length and variety of its Atlantic and Pacific coastlines, bizarrely the capital of US mainland windsurfing is a river. Wind is sucked through the steep sides of the Hood River in Oregon with such intensity that the locals had to invent a new adjective to describe it - 'nuclear'. The Gorge, as it's better known, is quite simply 'windsurf city'. It's a focus for competitions, manufacturers, test centres, schools and has spawned some phenomenal talent, Matt Pritchard and freestyle sensation Web Pedrick to name just two. On the east coast, Cape Cod and the Canadian Magdalen Island are just two of the destinations that have been catering increasingly for travelling windsurfers.

Maui – This Hawaiian Island has developed a reputation as the homeland of windsurfing. Constant warm winds and a powerful Pacific Ocean swell contribute to make this a windsurfing paradise. Without exception, the world's best live, train and develop their equipment on Maui. It exudes the sport through every pore. The beach is the social meeting point for teenagers, work buddies, wives and mothers. Everyone is involved. Everyone sails in Maui.

Along the north side of the island you can find conditions to suit everyone. Starting off at Kanaha, there are flat water as well as reef breaks to introduce the novice wave sailor to the delights and thrills of the island. Moving up the coast to 'Spreks' and 'Lanes,' a long stretch of peeling surf. But it's another three miles up the coast where true wave sailing reputations are won and lost. Ho'okipa Beach Park is the most famous wave sailing spot in the world. Most people are amazed to see the true scale of Ho'okipa. On first impressions it looks smaller than the pictures and videos suggest – until you get out there. Even on a relatively small six foot day, the speed and power of the waves demands another level of fitness and competence. But it's perhaps the knowledge that if you get it wrong, you'll be swept onto the infamous rock pile, that keeps all but the best, the bravest or most foolhardy on the beach. The seascape combined with the sheer brilliance of the action make Ho'okipa the world's most spectacular windsurfing location. Keep journeying along the coast for another couple of miles and you will reach Jaws – the biggest surfable and windsurfable wave on the planet. It's an outer reef that breaks perhaps a dozen times a year. It's the break that has made a thousand calendar shots and been the

cause of a thousand sleepless nights for the windsurfers who are irresistibly drawn towards its awesome scale and power. It's also jealously guarded by the locals – access by invitation only.

"A professional windsurfer's life is hard but I enjoy it. Most of the professionals have to travel so much on sponsor trips and promotions. Iballa and I, for example, have to do a lot of trips for sponsor photo shoots. We do get paid to do what we really love so this kind of travelling is really important to do. This is what takes us windsurfing in places like Maui, South Africa and Australia to name a few. We get to go to all these places for training, as well as for attending and competing in all the events." – **Daida**

The Atlantic – Off the north-west coast of Africa you'll find the Canary Islands. They benefit from the trade winds, which blow nearly all year round but are at their strongest during the summer months. Gran Canaria has a wide range of conditions on offer to suit most windsurfing levels. Pozo Izquierdo has earned its own reputation for strong winds – after a week of PWA competition the flags that line the beach front are usually reduced to thin shreds! Fuerteventura has played host to some of the most dramatic and spectacular race and speed events in the last twenty years. The miles of open sandy beach at Sotovento are already

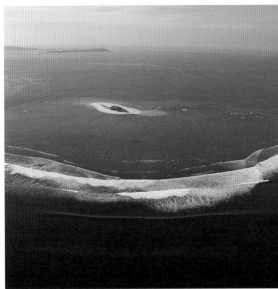

guaranteed a place in windsurfing history and continue to offer some of the best possible conditions for windsurfing tourists.

Ireland – The North Atlantic meets the west coast of Ireland with good news for windsurfers. Powerful swell, strong winds and a beautiful coastline have created a previously uncharted destination for windsurfers. In particular the Dingle Peninsular is developing a stellar reputation amongst the windsurfing community. The west coast is littered with secret bays and beaches waiting to be discovered by the windsurfing adventurer.

"This year's Ireland trip was great. It was my first windsurfing trip there. It is such a great place for cruising, sightseeing, drinking, and to my amazement the windsurfing was so good. I have been kicking myself ever since for not bothering to go over before. But believe me it isn't my last trip." – **Nik**

Northern Europe – Holland captures the pounding force of the North Sea, creating challenging conditions for the intrepid wave sailor. Likewise the German island of Westerland is equally exposed to the harsh and punishing waves of the North Sea and gripping winds that funnel up from the English Channel.

Southern Europe – Here there are warmer winds and warmer waters. Lake Garda in Northern Italy has hosted freestyle contests since the start of the new discipline. The thermal Ora wind funnelling between the mountains which rise along the side of the twenty-five mile stretch of water is ideal for more advanced sailors, blowing consistently each afternoon.

Spain – The Tramontana winds blowing across the Bay of Roses make the waters of the Costa Brava an ideal base for windsurfing, particularly for race and freestyle sailors. Where Africa meets Europe, the wind funnels through the narrow nine-mile gap between the continents to create one of the windiest spots in the world. The famous east 'Levant' wind has turned the quaint old Moorish fortress town of Tarifa into a windsurfing haven. Home to many World Cup races, slalom and speed events, it is Europe's most visited windsurfing destination. In the summer months, over 2000 boards have been counted in Tarifa's seven-mile bay.

As a general rule the summer winds in the Mediterranean are strongest in the east. Greece and Turkey are home to some great spots and cater for a variety of levels. The Meltemi winds arrive in the afternoon and with clockwork regularity blast between the islands.

"Life is short and I really try to enjoy everything that I'm doing now. I haven't actually travelled that much, (never enough!), but I do remember so many excellent places with very special people. I enjoy the events. It is true to say that I like to win, but that is obviously not always possible. Basically, the best part of my holidays are when I'm training and when I'm sailing." – **Daida**

Road trips
For many windsurfers, jumping in a van and heading off with some good friends is the best way to experience the best in the world of windsurfing. It's the freedom that can only be found on the open road. The emancipation of the soul.

" **the world is full of places waiting for windsurfers to explore** "

Top Left: "Dingle Bay in south west Ireland is somewhere I am certain to return." – Nik

Opposite: You can set your watch by the Meltemi wind in the Greek Islands.

The tradition of the road trip...

We meet at a predetermined rendezvous point in San Diego Airport. Here we hook up with the fleet of specialist off-road vehicles, which have been hired to deal with the rough terrain expected. We form a convoy and head for the Mexican border at the town of Tijuana. A quick break here, and the purchasing of more beer and supplies before we're back on the road. Destination: the heart of Baja.

It takes us twenty hours, travelling roughly due south. The solitary road is a track and is only kept clear by the singular vehicles that pass by every few weeks. It is un-navigable by any car or normal 4x4 – only high-suspension, full off-road vehicles can counter its roughness, pits and drop-offs. This is a cruise through a harsh region of the world as well as a meandering through the convoluted alleyways of the mind. Stunted bushes and a plethora of cacti surround the track. There obviously hasn't been a rainfall for a while, and great spumes of dust billow in to the still air, leaving a clear vestige of our path. It's windy, gritty and hot, the journey long and tempestuous. Storms are constantly brewing to the south, and the narrow-gauge road is hazardous. We're on the veritable road to nowhere for a solid twenty hours of bone-jarring bumps and vicious low-branch swipes. We pass along a rugged coastline with hidden coves, white sandy beaches, rocky bluffs and crystal-blue waters teeming with wildlife.

When we finally arrive exhausted we find nothing. We are fully prepared though, completely self-sufficient. We bring with us food and water, beer, cooking equipment, generators, porn, cookers, gas bottles and all our sailing equipment and set up camp. Our base camp is desolate to say the least. Our constant companion is a long, clean starboard tack wave, which reels along the beach providing one of the longest rideable waves in the world. Our other companions are scorpions and snakes and cacti, and lots of wide-open spaces and fresh air.

A summer tropical cyclone called a Chubascos comes spinning along the coast. It provides raw swell and accompanying strong onshores. We get the best conditions in the world. The sailing is unbelievable, and we spend long hours out amongst the waves and wind. But it is the territory that wins out in the awe-inspiring stakes.

This is the desert with very few trees and little shelter from the sun. It is steaming hot, the sand is baking and the heat shimmering. Rain does come in the form of the same summer cyclone. We are warned about flash floods. We are told not to bed down in riverbeds, advice we take as we re-pitch our tents on higher ground. We are surrounded by arid desert with stiflingly hot temperatures, yet we are afraid of flooding. We have also been warned about hurricanes, jellyfish stings, dangerous desert creatures and the more obvious threats like sunburn and dehydration. We ignore them all to go sailing. We are treated to excellent but exhausting mast-high waves, a steady breeze and waves that sometimes peel for two miles. This is it – the joy of the road trip realised.

Then the ocean goes flat. Having seen the shoreline from the perspective of the water for a while, a closer exploration is called for. It's a bit of a walk along a sand track, but the destination makes it well worth it. A broad vista encompasses a golden beach stretching into the hazy distance. Behind is a landscape of undulating savannah: tumbling dark clouds over to the north. It's quite away from the camp, and this short walk around the headland reveals another beach with a set of footprints on it. The footprints go on and on, yet there is no one on this unendingly stunning stretch of pristine sand.
The ocean is rumbling gently. Although the ocean is flat, she still moves languidly with a gentle, pacific motion. It is mildly hypnotic in its regularity. The consistent movement on the shoreline is indicative of a new swell approaching. The air is fresh. There is a wind out there.

We are lucky as sailors, getting to witness nature's beauty. We are living the dream. The road trip tradition lives on....

Above: Watching friends and checking out the competition is a great way to relax and a brilliant way to learn.

Opposite: A road trip with friends can be the best way to experience 'adventure sailing'. You and your buddies with a car load of gear. Sail when it's windy and drive on when it's not!

Below: Long days sailing uncrowded waves are a perk of the road trip.

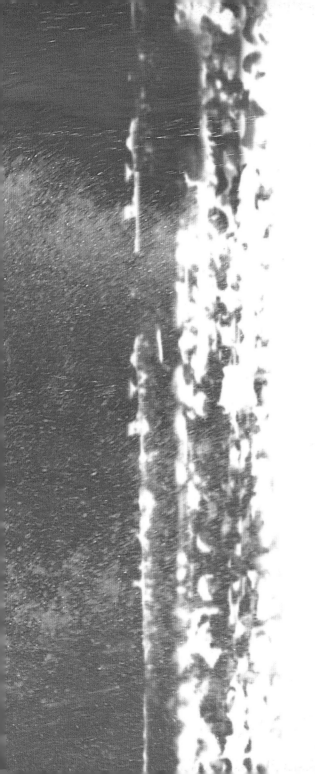

2

the equipment
question

"A professional windsurfer needs custom boards for wave sailing, because there are so many different places with a myriad of varying conditions. Windspeed and directions always differ. I have onshore boards (for places like Pozo or Sylt) and sideshore boards (for places like Maui). The wave sails are not nearly as complicated. My wave set goes from 2.8 square metres to 6.2, depending on the wind speed." – **Daida**

It must be quite clear now that windsurfers, particularly professionals, do not travel light. The impact that a fleet of windsurfers can have in an airport is fascinating, or terrifying, depending on which side of the check-in desk you stand. When ten or twenty sailors arrive together the equipment quickly mounts up. Before long you can have between one and two hundred boards, and an equal number of sails, masts and booms. Sometimes trucks are the best and the only way to move the circus from A to B.

"The only difficult part of travelling with gear is the airport. Firstly, you have to get it all to the airport for check-in, and then you have to be prepared to pay all the excess baggage fees. Sometimes the excess costs more than my standard ticket! But once again, as soon as I'm sailing, that's all forgotten and I feel myself again. I think we, as windsurfers will always be fighting for the right price for excess baggage. It's just part of the routine now." – **Daida**

To non-windsurfers we must appear fascinating creatures. We carry an odd assembly of kit in or on our cars. We arrive at the beach, regardless of the weather conditions, so long as it is windy. Manage to transform the odd assembly of boards and rigging into a precision piece of aerodynamic equipment that is exactly suited to the particular conditions and windspeed at that particular time and place. We then take off over the waves, returning a few hours later with a broad grin from ear to ear.

"I have a whole quiver of boards for the different disciplines. I've got three boards, of various volumes and lengths for Freestyle, and a whole quiver for Wave. These range from onshore to sideshore boards, small wave hotdog boards to Jaws big wave riding boards. About ten boards altogether. I still have two Old Faithful indoor boards for indoor competition. I like my boards to be fast, smooth and easy to use." – **Nik**

Above: At the end of the day it really is a case of who has the most toys.

Right: Checking that everything is properly locked in place can save you from problems out on the water.

27

Board design – rails and rockers

There are many different types of rockers, rails, bottom shapes outlines and combinations of the above. Basically it is rocker combined with a certain amount of bottom shape 'V' that makes the board smooth through the water, and makes it real easy to turn from rail to rail.

A hard rail with sharp lines will give you speed. A soft rounded rail will be easier to turn, but slow. The compromise is a tucked rail combining the qualities of both to a varying degree. A tucked rail will get you planing along nice and early AND allow for smooth turns. But the best play around with the set up of the sail, fin and mast foot position to complement their own personal style.

In onshore conditions where the waves are generally slow, choppy and gutless, the board, above all, has to plane early, accelerate and have a good top speed, not just for jumps but also to create a bit of dynamism and zip on wave faces that are shallow and aren't giving much back.

So it is that the onshore board will borrow a lot from slalom and speed designs. There won't be so much curve in the plan shape, the rails will be harder with a more pronounced edge which give a faster, cleaner, water release, which in turn means the board sits higher in the water, feels 'edgier' and more lively. A more upright fin will give increased lift to help you punch upwind out through the waves at the expense of a little manoeuvrability. Some also favour a wider tail, again for early planing, but also to give a better lift as you take-off.

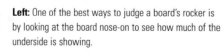

Left: One of the best ways to judge a board's rocker is by looking at the board nose-on to see how much of the underside is showing.

Opposite: The one handed spock is a competition favourite and a sure fired winner if you can pull it off in front of your friends!

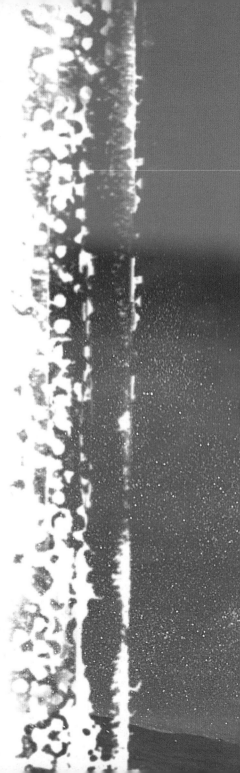

"As the waves can be either sideshore or onshore, we obviously have different boards for these conditions. The onshore boards normally have sharper rails than the sideshore ones, which have softer rails. I always want a fast board but obviously with full control as well. In Maui, for example, I really need a board that flies down the line as well as being easy for cutting back. The combination of speed and control is what we always look for. To test our boards and to develop them is really important for a professional windsurfer, although, when we are training we are always testing our own equipment and trying to get the best from it anyway. Once you've had a few custom boards you know in advance where the best position for the mast foot box and the fin box is. All that is left is to possibly change the fin size. You can also move it backwards or forwards depending on the conditions. The same applies for the mast foot." – **Daida**

"Sideshore boards are generally narrower, smaller, and thinner with softer rails. This is due to the fact that, while riding in sideshore winds, it allows you to use the speed and shape of the wave to build and maintain your speed. Therefore you need a board that is going to hold onto the wave at faster speeds while turning. The same principals apply to fins. A slightly softer, more raked fin is better for sideshore conditions. In good wave riding conditions, the wind is often light and gusty so you're not that bothered about jumping. So basically the sideshore board is just a surfboard with a sail." – **Nik**

" take **care of your kit** and it will take care of **you!** "

Freestyle and Freeride boards are both designed for use in a wide range of conditions and sail sizes. These are generally used in flatter conditions, utilising bigger sails. The main criteria for these boards are ease of planing and manoeuvrability. The rockers are straighter, and the outlines are rounder. These round rails keep the board smooth while turning, and give it a comfortable ride. Basically, we're trying to find the rockers, rails and outlines to make the boards fast planing, easy turning, smooth riding fun vehicles, for the widest possible range of conditions.

Above: With faith in your equipment you can go out and push it and yourself to the limits.

Right: Daida cranks on the downhaul.

Opposite: Fine tuning extends to the fin.

"The freestyle boards are different than the wave boards. They have flatter rockers so we can get up to speed faster in lighter conditions. These boards are bigger than the wave boards; they have more volume, and more area where you can move and 'dance' with more ease, particularly for 'freestyle.' " **– Daida**

Sails are unique for one reason – you can set them differently every time you go out. Sails cause the most problems for today's windsurfers, usually as a result of bad rigging. But there are NO excuses any more. Most of the modern designs come with a detailed rigging manual, detailing the exact out and downhaul setting for

under and over-powering winds and the recommended mast length and stiffness. Some even have markings on the sail to represent the centre of effort to help you set up your harness lines. But don't get too robotic about rigging. Manuals are good guides, but in the end you have to develop a FEEL for what's going on and then know which string to pull to make things better. As you crack along, the sensation should be that of the rig pulling evenly from one spot. As a gust hits, you should feel a steady pull followed by easy acceleration. In the gusts and lulls, the rig should 'breathe', the leech opening and closing to soften the sudden changes in pressure. The moment you have to wrestle with it, you're in no shape to do anything but survive, and that doesn't make for pretty viewing. The most common problem is a lack of downhaul. With no tension in the front of the sail, the centre of effort can move all over the place causing you to send irregular pulses of power into the board which will reward you by skipping, bucking and spinning out.

As you get better you develop preferences not only for the design of sail (and there are many ranges to choose from) but also for the way you like to set it up depending on your size and your sailing style. There are a wide range of sails available to meet most personal preferences and needs. In Daida's opinion, lightness and softness are the two words that describe the requirements for a good sail. She likes the sensitivity so that she can have better

control while sailing, and it also goes with the movement of her body. She feels that if she is sailing on a stiff sail her body cannot move, thus she can't turn as easily.

The selection of an appropriate mast is crucial. If the mast is too soft or too stiff, or if the bend of the mast doesn't match the curve of the luff (the leading edge), the sail will set like a crumpled crisp packet and you'll be going nowhere.

Opposite: Equipment is lighter now and the days of needing two people to carry your board down to the beach are long gone.

Above: Testing your equipment with a friend is a great way to tune up and ensure you enjoy maximum performance.

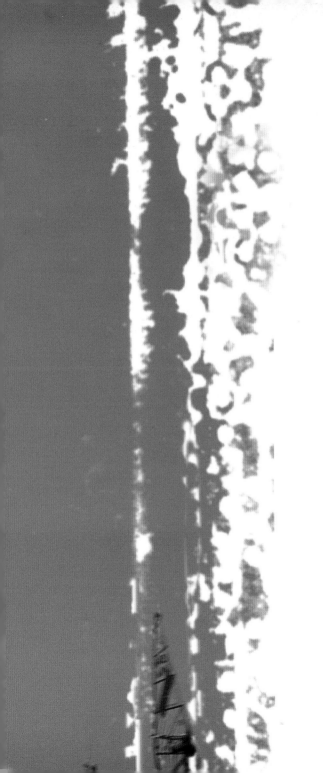

3
improving

Windsurfing requires a good level of fitness. As you continue tackling tougher conditions the physical demands will also increase. Yes, of course skill is more important but don't underestimate how much strength, fitness and agility are needed to survive the pounding of big waves or the force of a forty knot gust. Exhaustion can soon set in, particularly when swimming with equipment in heavy waves, a strong current or cold water. The trick is never to underestimate nature but always be realistic about your own limitations. A large part of the challenge is mental. Before you tackle nature you have to tackle the battle in your own mind and prepare yourself for that moment when you find yourself dropping in on your first big wave or going for that previously elusive manoeuvre. Like any situation in life, to improve you have to push yourself beyond your comfort zone. It becomes a question of whether you want to push yourself beyond that warm and cozy place in the search for success.

There is a certain protocol to follow when sailing in crowded places. Much of it is unspoken, until you break the rules and then, as you would expect, it becomes very vocal. In some locations, Ho'okipa for example, there can be a narrow channel in which to get out from the beach. It makes sense to pick your moment avoiding congestion, and the rocks. Once out and waiting for the wave, the simple unwritten rules of surfing come into play. Stated simply:

The person on the inside has the right of way, and once someone has caught a wave and claimed it, that person should have the right to surf the wave uninterrupted. In onshore conditions the wave will have more than one defined shoulder. In which case it's OK for a couple of sailors to share a wave but it's the one UPWIND who has right of way. Potentially the most severe collisions arise when the one surfing the wave meets the sailor trying to sail back out. In this situation it's the one on the wave coming towards the beach who has to take avoiding action.

Out of the breaking waves and we return to the old yachting rules. If two boards are on collision course on opposite tacks, it's the one with the wind coming from the right (on starboard tack) who has right of way. If you've both got the wind coming from the same side, then it's the one furthest upwind that has to steer clear. There are quite a few other rules but the over-riding one is to use a bit of common sense and give everyone a wide berth. After all, there's a good chance that the guy about to take you out doesn't know the rules anyway.

As your quest for adventure and challenging conditions increases so do the demands on your equipment. Good equipment care and preparation is essential. You have to have faith in your equipment as well as yourself. This might mean you need to invest in new kit but more importantly it's about understanding how to use and care for what you have. By spending time tuning and preparing equipment it is possible to save money and improve performance dramatically.

Sailing in stronger winds and bigger waves may mean you need smaller and perhaps more responsive boards and sails. Similarly, developing new freestyle moves might mean you need a board with different rail and rocker characteristics and more volume.

Opposite: Bernd Flessner squats down low as he starts to lean into the gybe.

Right: Antoine Albeau enters a gybe at full tilt. It's all or nothing at this speed. Notice how much of the board is actually in the water.

Early planing

One tip to give yourself a head start is to launch yourself positively from the beach. Push off and initiate some forward momentum. Keep your weight low with your head and shoulders right back to windward so you can see what's going on and stay committed against the rig. Stay loose and mobile, sail on your toes, make like a dancer and try and act like someone half your weight.

Timing the moment you hook in is essential. If the wind is marginal, stay out of the harness so you can hang off the rig and pump it to accelerate the airflow. If the wind is solid, then by hooking in straight away, you can use all your body weight to pull on the power rather than just your feeble arms.

The way to accelerate is to get your weight off the board. You do that by hanging away from the boom. As the board rises up, take delicate steps into the footstraps (front foot first). Remember that it's only when you're standing in the straps over the tail of the board that it can rise onto its minimum planing surface. Increasing your top speed is just about keeping the rig as still as possible so you don't upset the airflow, and about trimming the board. With the subtlest heel and toe pressure, you make sure that you're always presenting a flat surface to the water irrespective of waves and chop. The better sailors can 'see' the wind on the water, so they're already in position and anticipating the pressure changes before the gust hits. That's the way to plane early and overtake your mates.

Left/Opposite: Leave the beach with a positive push to help get the board moving forward and planing as early as possible.

Above: 1. Position the board heading downwind. **2.** Kick hard and step up. **3.** Keep the board balanced and your weight low. **4.** As you start to accelerate hook in and move into the straps.

Waterstarting

Done well this will save you time and energy and of course it's the only way to get going on small wave and freeride boards. Being able to waterstart quickly can be the difference between sailing away safely in between waves, or being washed onto the rocks.

The waterstart has two parts, the rig recovery and the start itself. To release the rig cleanly, you have to get it into a position where the wind can blow under it and do the work for you. Handle the rig from the mast tip, you'll have more leverage. Then swim with the mast so it's

" being able to **waterstart quickly** can be the difference between getting **away safely** or being **washed up on the rocks** "

roughly across the wind, raise it a little then throw it over your shoulder into wind like a javelin so air flows under the cloth and unsticks it from the water. With the sail up and flying, the rest of the move is just about getting the rig to produce enough power to lift you on. Start with the board across the wind and you at least a metre upwind of the upwind edge. Put your back foot on the board in between the footstraps; pull the tail of the board towards you at the same time throwing the rig forward and as upright as possible. By getting the rig high, you expose more of it to the wind and increase the power. But often that's not enough. YOU have to help the situation by making yourself an easy bundle to pull up. So like doing a forward roll, stay compact and roll your shoulders over your bent knees. In high winds keeping your weight low will help you to avoid an instantaneous catapult!

Or – imagine in your head that you are about to walk upstairs, with the only difference being that it only takes one step to get there. Use the mast as your walking stick, as it will help you to put all your weight in your front hand.

Tacking

One of the main advantages of a tack is that it will help you stay upwind. Even though a tack will lose you momentum, a gybe in the same situation will lose you a lot more ground. This makes tacking particularly useful whilst wave sailing or simply battling against wind and tide to get back to the shore.

Put your front hand on the mast, front foot in front of the mast foot, keeping bodyweight over the centre line of the board. Try to keep the foot switch to one quick movement. Rake the rig right back to give yourself some room and step round just before pulling the rig forward. Speed is the key; if you linger and start shuffling the

feet around, the board will stop and sink. Go into it with the aim of getting your feet around to the new side and the rig sheeted in on the new tack as quickly as possible. Watch the good guys tack a small board and it happens so quickly that the board barely drops off the plane.

Apart from keeping the feet away from the edges, the top tip is to bear away by throwing the rig forwards as you sheet in on the new side. Otherwise you'll stay head to wind and sink.

Below: (Left to right) **1.** Maintain your board speed as you start to head up into the wind. **2.** One foot in front of the mast and front hand on the mast ready for the quick switch. **3.** Try to make it one swift movement round the front. **4.** Take up your new foot position. **5.** Reach down the boom with the back hand and lean the mast forward to help you bear away. **6.** Get the board back on the plane and sail off on the new tack. Although you've lost speed, a quick tack will help you stay upwind far better than a gybe.

Gybing

Gybing is a move that frustrates half the population. It looks simple enough but there are actually a thousand things to co-ordinate in the space of about four seconds. Let's keep it simple. The main points are:

1. You have to have good planing speed with the feet in the straps.
2. You have to take that speed into the turn by keeping the rig sheeted in and powered up.
3. You have to carve a smooth and ever-tightening arc. With the back foot out of the strap on the inside rail, hold the rail in with constantly increasing pressure. Let the rail rise to the surface too early and you'll be swimming.
4. Keep the rig forward and flip it just after you've carved through the wind, and sheet in just off the wind on the new tack.
5. Switch the feet and step them forward of their respective straps to keep the board level as the sail swings round.

Nothing comes to those who hang back – especially not gybing. You have to lean further forward than you ever thought was sensible. If you don't, the acceleration as you carve downwind is such that it'll be like having the rug pulled from under your feet and you'll disappear out of the back door.

"I knew how to do a forward before gybing! A good tip is to look at the photographs, and study them again and again. It will be important to go downwind a bit, then press down on the board with your back foot for the turn. It will be easy to grab the sail on the other side." **– Daida**

Opposite: Racing gybe marks are not the place to meet new friends! A well-rehearsed fast gybe is the best tactic to employ and avoid trouble.

Right: Bjorn Dunkerbeck prepares for a gybe. Meanwhile see how the sailors behind are still low to the water, levering the sail over for maximum speed.

Speed

Eat more chips! Weight will always help to hold down a bigger sail and give you more forward momentum. Having said that, it's not just about lard. Look at Robert Teriitehau and Eric Thieme, both little blokes who rock in slalom and have been seen overtaking sailors 50kg heavier.

Speed is primarily about matching your kit to your size. Little people can get away with smaller boards, which create less resistance. They can't hold down as big a sail but they can make sure that sail is working perfectly for them. That means setting it on a soft mast with plenty of downhaul so it can deliver stable, efficient power even in the biggest gusts. From then on, speed comes from reading the wind and water to give board and rig the easiest ride. Keep the rig still and upright, at the same time playing with the sheeting angle, easing out the boom a few degrees as the gust hits and then

Left: The thrill of charging along at speed. The only sound is the wind rushing past your head and your board cutting through the water. Magical. – Daida

Opposite: Lucienne Ernst flat out speed and heading for the finish line.

gathering it in as the board accelerates. Always look ahead to pick the easiest route between the waves and chop. In big chop, let the board ride up under soft knees like a skier through the bumps. In smaller chop, keep tension through the legs to plaster the board to the water. In marginal winds hang off the boom a little more to let the board rise up onto the fin and achieve that wonderful sensation of just sliding through the water.

Stay square onto the power source, keep the shoulders parallel with the boom, sheet in, grit the teeth and take no prisoners!

4
dancing
with waves

The sea in all her moods can be a dazzling display of nature's beauty as well as a harsh example of her cruelty. She can howl like a banshee as well as have her moments of unparalleled beauty. The waves she produces are our playing fields, our medium for expression. What we do on these waves is entirely dependent on what our imagination conjures up.

All progress in a sport of adventure, an adrenaline sport, is based on imagination. What the mind can conjure up, the body and board can do. We push ourselves in waves of consequence because our emotions run free and tell us, in moments of madness, that impossible situations are completely possible. Just a few years ago the Cheese roll (a forward somersault) was an impossible dream, a ludicrous cartoon move that was doomed to exist in the minds of free-thinkers of our sport. That was until Cesare Cantagalli came along and pulled it off, surprising all including himself. In the process, he let open the veritable flood gates of advancement – as soon as the mental block was erased the future of new moves was blown wide open. Nowadays we have the double forward; a previously inconceivable move, pulled off on fairly regular occasions. The concept of wave riding is something that is incredible to comprehend. We harness the power of the waves beneath us and the wind in our sails to achieve the closest man can come to flying, at one with nature and the world of energy around us.

The act of riding waves is extremely empowering. It has in the past been compared to bullfighting or firewalking. It is truly remarkable that a human being can have such control over high seas as well as human emotions. The feelings of exhilaration and of release, the

Left: Daida glides through a backloop high above her hometown of Pozo.

Opposite: Josh Angulo takes off for another giant floater.

unadulterated whoop of joy, the primal scream of sheer excitement are the rewards for venturing out into our mother ocean. Once you have learned to deal with the combined power of waves and wind and can harness this power to the full advantage of your equipment, then you are well on your way to windsurfing consummation. Yet it is a rocky, narrow path and the sea will throw a few curve balls before you get close to understanding. You see, the variables are too great, and you can never fully master this complex pastime.

"I started windsurfing because of the waves. I was surfing all the time before windsurfing and here in Pozo we had wind all the time, so wind and waves were the reason. I started right here in 35 knots of wind and I got absolutely trashed so many times, hundreds of times. I still get trashed. I always say that if you want to do something you've got to try it first, and it's not easy. At the end you learn from your mistakes, like life in general."
– **Daida**

"Basically I did most of my sailing on the south coast of England, and whenever the winds were good and strong we would get fun little waves to ride and jump. That was my start. I then started travelling on family holidays to the Canaries which has some great wave sailing spots for all kinds of levels, and it went from there."
– **Nik**

Shorebreaks

Shorebreaks are the windsurfer's Nemesis. They can be brutal, destructive and can turn thousands of pounds worth of exotic equipment into matchwood in a matter of seconds. When a wave runs suddenly into very shallow water it folds over itself and 'dumps'. Relentless wave action tends to pile sand or stones high at the beach head, creating a shelf, so shorebreaks are inevitable on beaches unprotected by reefs that face out into the open ocean. To get out into the waves beyond, you have to bite the bullet and sometimes learn by bitter experience. However, most breakages can be avoided by being smart and keeping a cool head.

First take a moment to observe the whole picture. Because of the changing shape of the beach, the waves may not be breaking so fiercely a hundred yards downwind. In deep water channels (created by streams of retreating water) there may be no shorebreak at all.

OK, so it's crashing everywhere. Your next tactical weapon is timing. Wait by the waterside and observe the rhythm of the waves. Often there'll be a lull in proceedings – that, of course, is the time to make a dash for it. Speed is your best weapon. The impact zone may only be 30 yards out, so the quicker you can make it beyond that point, the quicker you're out of danger. So as soon as you drop your board in the water, you have to step on, sheet in and pump the rig with every sinew to make that ground. Hold board and rig high above your head. Stand upwind of everything and hold the mast with the front hand and the front footstrap with the back hand. Stand in about knee deep water, wait for the wave to break, let it wash through you and then launch onto the back of it before the water retreats again. Remember that the shorebreak is sucking all the water up in front of it. So get the timing wrong and launch in front of it and you'll find yourself on exposed sand staring into the jaws of a pitching monster.

" to get out into the **wave beyond** you have to **bite the bullet...** and sometimes learn by **bitter experience** "

Opposite: Daida does battle in heavy Irish shorebreak.

Left: Good speed and confidence is essential when launching into a forward loop. You can't go gently! – Daida

c) The fin, of course, offers no resistance in the air, so the board's direction is controlled with a scissors action of the legs. To stop the tail spinning off downwind, stretch out the front leg and pull the back foot up under the bottom to bear away and land slightly off the wind.
d) Most importantly, take things in bite sized chunks, don't bite off too much too soon. You'll come off worse! Once you have the techniques wired you can move on to bigger waves and bigger air!

"How do you go about doing your first basic jump? When I first started jumping I had actually just learned how to waterstart, and then I learned how to hook onto the harness and get my feet in the footstraps. It was only afterwards that I started concentrating on my jumping. I used to utilise every chop to learn how to jump. In every reach I tried to jump at least five times before I fell.

"Then I would go back to the beach and try again. Keep on trying the same things over and over 'til I was getting higher and higher, and then I would try something different in the air. I learned to do forwards before I could gybe 100 percent." **– Daida**

Basic jumping

Jumping is something we all love to do, and it is also one of the most visually appealing things that initially attracts most people towards windsurfing. It is such a remarkable feeling, gliding above everything out there. For first time wave-jumpers, the main things to remember are to:

a) Try and hit the waves straight on.
b) Sail the board through the air. Sheet in on take-off for maximum lift but then control the power and angle of the board by sheeting in and out. Sheet out to cut the power and come down tail first. Sheet in to go for a nose first landing or, ultimately, a forward loop!

Basic riding

On a wave you have two basic options: to ride it upwind with your back to the wave (backside) or to ride it downwind facing the wave ('down the line' or frontside). Which you choose will depend on the wind direction, which way the wave is peeling and how good you are. For your first attempts, backside is a whole lot easier. Riding upwind you're not going so fast and it's much easier to control the speed and power. The perfect beginner conditions are a cross onshore wind so that your natural reaching course takes you along the wave face and crumbly, two to three foot wind blown waves that won't destroy board and rider if things go wrong.

There are no rules. Your basic aim is to make a series of tight and long turns along the wave face and tap into its power to lend those turns a bit of dynamism.

Three main points for basic riding.

a) Try to remain on or as close to the wave as possible, as this will help keep your speed up. The most powerful section of the wave is by the shoulder, just in front of where the wave is breaking. This is where you'll pull off your most powerful moves.

b) Be totally mobile. There are such sudden changes in speed and direction that you have to anticipate with radical shifts of weight from front to back foot. In a downwind bottom turn for example, you have to lean right forward to engage the whole rail. Then, as you climb the face and prepare to turn on the top of the wave (the top turn or 'off-the-lip') and redirect the board down the face, you shift all the weight to the back foot and the upwind rail.

Above: (Right to left) **1.** Sail towards the wave with speed to help you carve round without stalling. **2.** Adjust your carving angle to stay in front of the wave. **3.** As you carve, start planning your angle down the wave. **4.** As you flip the sail the wave will start to carry you forwards. **5.** You are now in a position to start your turns along the wavelength.

c) That mobility extends to the rig. Although basically you're surfing, it's those who exploit the rig's power at the right moment that produce the most powerful performances. Watching Robby Naish for example, you see his back hand reach right down the boom so he can sheet in harder into the bottom turn. He then slides it forward as he climbs the face so it's in a better position to pump the sail as he drives off the back foot in his top turn. The result? The wave just shatters underneath him in an explosion of spray.

The rinse cycle (handling a crisis)

When approaching waves for the first time, remember to take it nice and easy.
Don't go straight out into mast-high surf, get yourself into trouble straight up, and put yourself off forever. Ask people who are sailing what the particular area is like regarding currents and conditions.
Also, always sail with a few friends.

A few thing to remember:

Firstly, try to always be wave-side of your gear when you are about to get trashed by a wave.

Secondly, the power of the wave is in the top so sink the rig as deep as you can and usually the wave will break harmlessly over it. If you decide to hang on to your rig, try to do it by holding the mast just above the boom instead of holding it high up towards the tip. It thus has less chance of breaking.

Thirdly, always try to stay with your gear as it can act as a life raft if you're injured or out of breath.

Lastly, remember that some wipe-outs are really serious. They are going to happen, it is inevitable. It is important to understand the cycle of a big wipe-out in order to know how to deal with them. Wipe-outs are not nice. No one likes to be held under water for a long time.

The average hold-down is extremely fleeting, but because of the severe bodily thrashing and the activity all around you underwater, the time period is extremely exaggerated. It is usually only a few split-

Below: When a wave takes you, there's no point fighting back. You're in for the ride!

seconds before you are released to pop back up to the surface for a huge lung-full of sweet, life-giving air. It is very easy to test how long you can hold your breath underwater for, in a pool or some other controlled environment. Also, it is possible for extremists to expand their lung capacity by practising holding their breath underwater. Most people can swim underwater for 45 seconds and many can swim for a whole lot longer.

So, time yourself in the safety of a pool sometime, and the knowledge of your lung capacity will give you so much more peace of mind when sailing in big conditions.

If you're getting thrashed around and you realise that it's actually only a matter of seconds that you are really going to be underwater for, it will help to keep you much calmer.

Another thing to remember clearly when involved in a savage wipe-out and hold-down, the wave's energy is infinitely stronger than yours is. There is no way that you can fight against the energy of the ocean. Finally, "try and count slowly to yourself when being held underwater. It might put all things into perspective." – **Nik**

"Once I came pretty close to drowning. Well, I've probably been close a few times, but it doesn't really worry me. It makes me just want to go sailing and try again. What happened was I got hooked under the sail, and the waves were pushing my sail down and I couldn't get out. I was trapped under the sail and still hooked on the harness and couldn't breathe. It was quite bad. It never happened again though because I learned from my mistake – I just needed to unhook before the gybe." – **Daida**

Getting into the rhythm of the waves

Watch a good wave sailor on his home patch and it's uncanny how he always seems to be in the right spot at the right time. On the way out, he always hits the wave just before it peaks so he launches into the wildest jumps. On the way in, he always takes off on the biggest wave of the

set exactly where it's peaking. And he never seems to get caught out. Even when he wipes, he gets out of there without being trashed by the next set. He's not in touch with a greater being, he's just in rhythm with the ocean. He's aware of the banks and reefs, so knows where the waves are likely to peak. He knows where the channels are, so he can find a safe route back out where the waves aren't breaking; and after a zillion hours of sailing in that spot, he has accumulated a huge amount of information which just allows him to operate instinctively.

The best advice is to sit on the beach and watch the waves. Take as long as is needed. Count how many waves are in a set. Time the frequency of the waves – how often they are coming through. Often the second and third waves are the best waves of a set; but then again this also could vary. The other thing is, once you're out the back

of the breaking waves, be patient and let a couple of sets go through before you select a wave for yourself. Another top tip is to go surfing. This really helps your timing and understanding of the waves. So, when there's no wind and you're just hanging around on the beach – go surfing. It's fun.

Above: Jason Polakow bottom turns through the white-water at Ho'okipa taking the chance to plan his next move.

Opposite: Francisco Goya looks down the line of the wave. The first bottom turn will set you up for the wave and is a chance to judge how it might break.

Staying upwind

After you have ridden the wave to its completion, and all that is left is whitewater, you should try to get a head start on getting upwind by riding the whitewater upwind as far as you can. Then try to tack rather than gybe, as a gybe will inadvertently result in you losing about thirty-foot downwind.

To sail upwind on a small board, you must have speed. The small, sweptback wave fin doesn't offer much lift, so the technique is to plane fast, then carve gently upwind until you feel yourself stalling; then bear away again and repeat the process so you're looping upwind. Your most potent aid is the wave itself. Just stay on the face, point upwind and use it like a conveyor belt.

If the waves are coming through in slow, irregular lumps, the trick is to plot a course through them so you're always sailing downhill, luffing up when you're on a swell, bearing away to overtake and catch the next. Soon that embarrassing walk back up the beach to your start point will be a thing of the past.

Opposite: My friend Jason Polakow demonstrates his powerful style with a sweeping cutback right along the lip of the wave. – Nik

Right: Jennifer Henderson carves across the top of a wave with the lip just starting to peel behind her.

5
taking it to the limit

literally is the limit. What was dreamed about years ago as impossible to pull off is now commonplace, and where does it lead? Where does technology end? Well, we are not going to find out in this lifetime. We are here to push the boundaries on a daily basis, to turn the impossible into the distinctly possible, and to keep on expanding our mental grasp of progression, because progression, be it in life, in sport, or in the amazing turns we can learn to pull off on waves of the future, is absolutely endless.

Wind tips

Your general performance, how you ride the wave and the moves you go for always depends on the wind direction. Ireland is a good example of a destination where the wind direction changes all the time.

"One day it was onshore, (blowing from the sea to the land) so jumps score higher with the judges. Coming back in you tend to ride the wave backside, but if you can ride it frontside (downwind) you'll score more, because in onshore winds it's very hard. It's difficult to control the power in the sail and you lose a lot of ground downwind. Generally onshore winds blow in at a slight angle from the left or right (where I sail at Pozo on Gran Canaria, they blow from the left). When the wind blows straight onshore, this is the worst as it's really difficult to get out through the waves." **– Daida**

Above: Jaws is the most awesome big wave spot I have ever seen or sailed – Nik

Opposite: Francisco Goya launches into a wave 360. Using all his speed to drive through the move and letting the power of the wave keep pushing him forward.

When it comes to the outer limits of what can be achieved in the waves, the limits have only ever been set by the length and breadth of the human imagination. Since man first launched a board into the surf in the early seventies, the push has been relentless and there's no indication that the progress chart is levelling out. With equipment being so much lighter, faster, more manoeuvrable and giving so much more control in extreme situations, the sky

Onshore winds

Even if a good swell is running, the effect of onshore winds is to make the ocean look a bit of a mess. Often it's just a cauldron of white water with waves tumbling all over the place in no discernible pattern. The onshore wind blows the waves over before they have a chance to build, so the faces are 'mushy', shallow, and less powerful. They're still loads of fun though, if you choose the right gear. Don't get too hung up on design. The one word on your mind should be 'big' - a big board to help you float over the white water, give you acceleration between the tightly spaced waves; and also a big rig to give you power to get upwind and punch through the whitewater (check chapter 2 for more design details). Whether you're in competition or just free sailing, staying upwind is probably the most important skill. Onshore winds tend to set up a downwind current inshore so you're always losing ground, especially if you fall. If you have confidence in your ability to sheet in and point up, you'll have no worries about giving it your all; if not, you'll spend your whole time trying to edge back to your starting point and will go nowhere.

Sideshore

This is the ideal direction for wave performance; perfect for jumping in that you're reaching straight out through the waves at full speed and perfect for riding, in that the angle leaves you free to ride up or downwind.

Blowing from the side, the wind can produce a little cross chop on and in front of the wave faces but it doesn't blow them down and make them break prematurely. As a result they tend to be faster, steeper, cleaner and more powerful. Ho'okipa Beach, Maui is the perfect example of a predominantly sideshore break. With conditions being altogether more conducive to jumping, riding and simply getting out through the break, you can go for more dedicated wave equipment.

"In sideshore conditions I tend to set my sail a little flatter and even use a smaller sail at times. Board-wise, you can use a narrower board and smaller fin, as you can use the power of the wave to help keep you planing at speed while wave riding, and thinner rails, as you are going faster into your turns. Thinner rails will help to keep it buried in the water while turning." – **Nik**

Onshore winds signal the time for jumping. Winds off the sea are always more constant and the shallower face of the onshore wave actually makes the perfect take-off ramp for beginner and expert alike. The key to a dynamic performance, as well as being the way to stay out of trouble, is to maintain planing speed. If you drop off the plane in breaking surf, you are that rabbit caught motionless in the headlights of a speeding truck. You head up a few degrees to hit the wave head on, but then bear away on landing to power up again. It's the same when riding back in. Watch the guys who really rip in the onshore stuff, and they punctuate long fast lines with sudden explosions. By pumping the rig and working the wave with shallow turns, they generate the speed to pull off the big moves in apparently 'dead' situations.

" boundaries are limited only by a rider's imagination "

Cross offshore

The effect of an offshore wind on the waves is astounding. Suddenly there's no chop (there's no space for it to build up) and the effect of the wind blowing against the faces, holds them up, making them steeper and more hollow, so that when they do break, the lip throws over and breaks with huge power. So what are your options when the wind is blowing diagonally from land to sea?

Your first problem is just getting out. Offshore winds are always gusty, especially inshore and around the impact zone. As you approach a big wave, the wave itself acts like a barrier to the wind, leaving you sinking in a hole just when you need maximum power. Getting out requires excellent balance, (for often you

are off the plane) combined with exquisite timing and wave sense. Wait for a set to come through and then make your bid for the outside.

Jumping in offshore winds is a bit of a nightmare. You have to take-off on a broad reach and with the wind from behind, it's hard to control the power. Often you get sent into an involuntary forward loop. The wind gets squeezed up the wave face so you get a massive gust at the top as you take-off but then land in a lull. Most look to avoid jumps and just concentrate on riding.

This is THE direction for frontside, down-the-line riding – perhaps the most exciting of all the windsurfing options. As you bear

Opposite: Power with style results in a spectacular show.

Above: Wind power...

Below: When the whitewater closes in around you. Hang on, you might still make it!

off down the wave, you have the wind from the side, your most controlled point of sailing. Then as you bottom turn and climb the face, the rig is at its most powerful, so you can exploit that force as you turn off the top of the wave, to launch

into the big aerial off-the-lip. It's in cross-offshore winds that you see the biggest and wildest wave-riding moves. But before we get carried away, just let the voice of doom have a quick word. What happens if something breaks? Surely you'll just get blown straight out to sea never to be seen again? There's a heavy safety consideration in any kind of offshore wind. You have to be a very competent windsurfer to even consider it, confident in your ability to sail upwind, to crawl home semi-submerged if the wind drops and in your fitness to swim board and rig back if you have a problem. The rules are:
1) Never go out alone. 2) Stay close to shore within the wave break, then if you do have a problem, you can body surf back to shore.

Above: (Left to right) The double forward is performed with varying levels of success. Francisco landed this with his own smooth chilled out style and grace.

Left: Taking a slice off the top of the wave.

As far as kit is concerned you take out the smallest most manoeuvrable board you can get away with. Some favour a low boom so they can drop into a lower surfing stance and keep the board underneath them when they cut back. Rig selection is an interesting problem. On big days, you can drift out off the plane totally under-powered but then turn round, catch the wave and find yourself unable to hold on. You are a victim of 'apparent wind'. The wave is perhaps moving at 15mph, which then combines with the true wind to produce something altogether more powerful. On the way out you may have been sailing in a Force 3 but on the wave face it's a Force 6 – that's why you see the good guys wallowing out with rigs that LOOK far too small for the conditions.

Big move tips

Big height in jumps comes less from sheer speed and more from hitting the wave at exactly the right spot, and having maximum power in the rig. Keep an eye on the wave and gauge your speed so you smack the lip just as it's starting to curl over. Feather the sail as you climb the face and then sheet in hard just as the tail of the board leaves the lip. It's an explosive moment where every sinew works on projecting the board upwards. The front foot kicks up and forwards, the back foot lifts the board high under the backside like a plane retracting the undercarriage. The arms throw the rig up and forwards on take-off and then bring it down laterally over the head so it acts like a wing to project the force upwards rather than forwards. Lift the windward edge with the heels so the wind can get under the board and float it even higher. Big wind will give you much bigger jumps than a big wave. Who will ever forget Bjorn Dunkerbeck getting 40 foot of air off head-high waves at Pozo, but he did have 50 knots of wind! Landing from rocket air is a worry. The safest way is to sheet out at the top of the jump, let the board drift a little upwind and then float down tail first. If ever you bear away off the wind when you're up there, you'll be straight into a potentially face-planting nose-dive....or perhaps a forward loop.

"what we previously thought of as limits are now a distant memory"

Right: The back loop.

Below: Daida launches into action.

The forward loop

"Start off on a smaller wave at first, so it won't be a big problem if you go around and land on your back the first few times. It's good to just get the feeling. Sail at a wave full-speed because if you slow down before take-off you get more wind into your sail and the rotation can get a lot more violent. Move your back hand as far back as possible and, as you take-off, roll your front shoulder forwards – towards the mast sheet. Pull your ankles up towards your bum and you will roll over nice and easy. Once again, you should also be able to look behind your back elbow and see a landing spot." **– Nik**

The back loop

Psychologically the back loop is a lot easier to go for, because you're always upwind of your equipment and in a position to bail out. However, it's harder to land cleanly. The mistake many make is going for it like a bull in a china shop but actually it should be a very slow and easy rotation. Take-off as if you were doing a normal high, vertical jump. At the apex of the jump, sheet out and the nose will drift towards the wind. Then just by looking back over your front shoulder and looking for your landing, you'll keep the rotation going and if you're lucky, you'll land the right way up. A lot of people try to force the spin by sheeting in at the top, but you then rotate so fast that you've no chance of controlling the landing. Looking at the landing spot is probably the most important piece of advice you can get.

Aerials without injury!
"I have no idea! Other than don't try it on a massive wave or a really shallow reef." - **Nik**

"Aerials without injury! I know that you need to get the timing right. It's actually all about timing when doing an aerial. Your body position is really important. There are real sudden changes of direction so you have to anticipate with the body. Throw your body into it, stay powered up and let the power of the wave take you to the end." – **Daida**

Also, to make the most out of a wave, you want to do as many good, fast, powerful turns as possible. To do this you have to be in the most critical part of the wave, which means you have to be as close as possible

to the curling whitewater but still be on the clean open face. Wave riding is actually quite a science. There are so many styles and even more manoeuvres. To make the most out of a wave you also need to concentrate on moving your body all the time. It actually is a lot like dancing. Not everybody dances the same, and to dance better you have to go dancing often. With regards to the various styles, the New School style developed mainly by the young Jason Polakow in the early nineties borrowed a lot from skateboarding – lots of tight slashing turns on the face, often breaking the fins out and sliding the board around using shorter wider boards. The Old School, meanwhile is a lot more 'carvy' - long, fast bottom turns using the whole edge of a longer, narrower board,

into powerful, deep, off-the-top turns. Lots of positive edge to edge turns, really tapping into the wave's most powerful sections. It remains the style of the best big wave riders.

"From watching videos and reading old magazines I could see a huge difference in styles. As the equipment developed, so the styles in general have changed. For example, Josh Angulo has a unique style; nobody does what he does. It looks like he doesn't use his hips to 'dance' the wave, but he is an incredible wave rider, one of the best. I think that equipment development paved the way for style changes, and also helped to develop more manoeuvres, especially in freestyle." – **Daida**

Big surf

When you're out there, amongst immense waves and there is a possibility that your life could be in danger, it is a strange fact that inconsequential things in your life so quickly become just that – inconsequential. You are not in any way worried about bills and shopping and mortgage payments and approaching deadlines – it's just you, your rig and a massive towering mountain of angry, foaming wave bearing down on you.

A couple of million years of progress have let the human body invent a refined system for recognising menacing situations and dealing with the fear. We as humans have gotten so good at dealing with danger that we have all but eliminated risk from our lives. Where our ancestors faced woolly mammoths, floods and plagues and threat and danger as part and parcel of daily survival, we contemporary humans have all but beaten the natural world and eliminated danger. Where we were brilliant and creative in eliminating danger, now we are equally creative in inventing it. Simulating fear is why people go sky diving and climb Mount Everest and BASE jump off high rises in crowded cities. Simulating fear is why guys like Nik and Anders Bringdal and other unbalanced people sail out to sea to try and conquer waves like Jaws when most of us just want to look the other way.

The reason? Stated quite simply, fear is good. A substantial dose of unfeigned fear is soothing to the human psyche and the human body. When the brain detects a dangerous predicament, it sends out a red alert to every tissue, organ and sense in the body. The agent is a chemical called norepinephrine, which is closely coupled to adrenaline, a hormone secreted from two glands on top of either of the kidneys. This chemical works as lubrication for the brain and body. It loosens up the nerve synapses and speed impulses from the brain to all receptors and back again. Norepinephrine explains some of the dialect of windsurfing. The 'gut wrench' you get when experiencing or witnessing a heavy situation is norepinephrine blasting stomach tissues. The 'head rush' you get when making a big drop is actually norepinephrine rushing to your brain to help you evade that situation.

When the brain detects fear it sends norepinephrine to every part of the body and keeps sending it until the menace has passed. The body and the brain enjoy being on alert because it feels so grand. And the after effects are pleasing too. Dopamine, a chemical by-product of norepinephrine is left behind in the brain for hours after a formidable predicament. Dopamine is often interpreted as elation. The ebullience can last for hours and even days after a tremendous Jaws session. The stimulation of fear and its after-effects are as habit-forming as any substance or activity on earth. And like addiction, once you've had a taste, there's just no going back.

Above: Anders Bringdal stays ahead of the monster.

"The nastiest moments of my life sailing have obviously been in Ho'okipa. I started sailing here in Pozo and it was a huge difference in conditions from here to there. I went from port tack side-on winds to side-off starboard wind, and with real waves. Well that's where I had all my nastiest accidents. The reef and the rocks in Ho'okipa are waiting for all the new comers, and I was one. I think I almost died there. I think I need some more time in starboard conditions to go and sail Jaws, but I guess Nik has some stories over there, eh?" **– Daida**

"Jaws is the most awesome big wave spot I have ever seen or sailed. In some ways it is easy to sail as there is always a channel, and you can ride the shoulder of the wave in a safe area. On the other hand, if you get it wrong and get caught by a west peak or simply wipe-out in the pit, you are going to be down for a long, long time and you are going to be really deep. Thankfully I have not yet experienced that at Jaws and hopefully I won't get it too bad in the future. The rush of sailing down such a huge amount of water at such high speed knowing that a little mistake could be your last is awesome and incredibly scary at the same time." **– Nik**

" it's just you, your kit and a massive towering mountain of angry foam "

the freestyle
phenomenon

"I think freestyle is great. You just need one board and three sails to practice with, and it's pretty accessible to everybody. It's also really fun, because we used to sit around waiting for waves to jump and surf, but what about those flat days? Now I can always have fun, in all kinds of conditions.

In waves, you wait until you get a ramp or jump, but in freestyle you are moving and doing manoeuvres all the time, whenever you get some planing. There is a larger variety of manoeuvres than in waves, yet it is as radical as wave sailing." **– Daida**

What started as a bit of harmless showing off, has since turned into the third professional discipline on the World Tour and what a breath of fresh air it is! Freestyle has brought the thrills and spirit of wave sailing to flat water and opened the door for sailors with limited funds, many of whom live and train on lakes, to break into the tour and start winning. Music to the travelling windsurfer's ears is that compared to the racer with his mountains of finely tuned, feather light and hugely expensive kit, the freestyler can compete at top level with a couple of production boards and rigs.

In competition, freestyle is about stringing together a winning routine in front of a panel of judges. They're looking for flow, imagination and originality. But above all it's about fun and for that very reason it has been easy for the discipline to translate from competition to recreational sailing.

Freestyle has many influences and the complete performer, such as Barbadian Brian Talma, who draws his routine from many sources. There are the Old School long board tricks such as body pirouettes and rig spins; there are modified wave sailing moves such as spin loops and carving 360s, and there is the New School wizardry. Spurred on by the spirit of skate and snowboard, pioneers such as Josh Stone and Robby Seeger have developed an array of tendon twisting moves such as

the Spock, Vulcan and Willy Skipper. Which tricks they do depends on the windstrength and water conditions.

Recently, there is evidence of freestyle moves migrating back and being integrated into wave sailing. On the Canarian island of Fuerteventura for example, the PWA freestyle final is held in

Opposite: Success in freestyle doesn't come easy, but it's fun learning.

Below: Freestyle has revealed some of the most spectacular and dramatic windsurfing images imaginable.

Left: Nik shows how to bend the rules.

Below: The speed loop – Daida shows how. It's all over in the blink of an eye!

small waves, so you're not only marked on your riding and jumping but on everything you do in between. You'll see body drags, sail and body 360s and even Spocks (a 360 planing spin on the nose) being performed on the wave itself. You'll see loops on the way out AND on the way in, one footed jumps, no handed jumps, rail grabs as well as a thousand variations of the standard tacks and gybes. For sure, freestyle has brought a new energy to wave sailing and it has given recreational sailors worldwide new and exciting challenges that they can now tackle wherever they sail.

The best news for all is that freestyle has spawned the development of some magnificent new equipment. A freestyle board has to plane early, accelerate well and spin on a sixpence. But above all, it has to be stable and forgiving so that it helps you recover from the wildest situations. These are qualities that help everyone whether you're looking to nail that first Vulcan or survive your first basic gybe. Not surprisingly freestyle designs now account for nearly a third of all new equipment purchased worldwide.

The boards are basically short and fat so the volume is concentrated just where you need it – under your feet and the mast foot. The combination of straight rocker and soft rails make it perform like a big, fast wave board. Freestyle sails favour acceleration over top speed. A tight leech and relatively flat profile make them rotate easily in tacks and gybes and make them light and easy to handle during the sail tricks. Freestyle has helped to simplify the market, and has provided a new and dynamic direction for the sport.

Before launching yourself into the world of freestyle sailing you need to get yourself into a mentally free zone. Freestyle requires you to bend the rules and develop new ways of thinking. It is also a physically demanding experience and takes you back to those early days of throwing yourself about and wondering when it was all going to start making sense.

The good news is that there are no real rules. Freestyle, like wave sailing, is essentially about self-expression. Variation and individual style is what makes freestyle so exciting and appealing, whether you are entertaining your friends or the judges in a World Tour Championship.

" **freestyle**, like wave sailing is essentially about **self-expression** "

There are many different, but equally valid approaches to learning a new trick. Some like to hide themselves away and plug away at it alone with no peer pressure, others like to train as a group and feed off each other. However, most importantly you must have a clear idea of what you're trying to achieve by either watching someone do it or, better still, by replaying a video time and time again, imagining yourself as the performing sailor. The approach thereafter depends on the trick itself. Some, like say the helicopter tack,

are easy to break down and practise in bits. You can get a hang of the sail spin on dry land, then try it on a floaty board in light wind and finally work up to the real thing. For the faster planing tricks like the spin loop, Spock or Vulcan which are all over in a second, you just have to give it a go, crash and burn and build up a bank of responses that allow you to get a bit further each time.

"The best approach to improving is to just repeat the manoeuvres over and over. To

have an open mind and learn from your mistakes. If you have no idea how to do a forward, for example, just ask someone who knows how to do it and then dream with it, have it in mind day and night, and then try it. As soon as you try, you'll probably see your mistake and you'll do it better next time... be repetitive!" – **Daida**

Spock
"You have to be going full speed. The jump part of the manoeuvre should be off the flattest part of water there is, as this

will stop the tail of the board going up and over. If this happens, the tail will sink and you'll land on your ass. So, do it off flat water, and spin the board around. This way you will keep your forward momentum and have a better chance of pulling it off. Also, grab the mast sleeve with your old back hand/new front hand and keep your body weight really low down, below the boom. Then, lean your weight onto the back part of the sail to force it around." – **Nik**

"I do not find this an easy manoeuvre. For the Spock you need to come downwind a bit and do a Vulcan planing backwards. It will be easier to put your back hand on the mast. Keep that hand in front of your face as you are doing the rotation, with the other hand on the sail. Look to your back and put your weight in your front foot to spin the fin and rotate easier. Despite the difficulty, the Spock is my favourite move." – **Daida**

Left: (Left to right) Richie Foster performs a Spock. Variations on the popular moves are what help to make freestyle so exciting.

Above: Ben Van Der Steen goes over the top.

Right: The 'Shove it' is just one move that can be performed both in the waves and in flat water freestyle.

"...most of my moves are by accident..."
– Nik

"I have to practise everything all the time before it comes out. It has never happened to me that I've done a new move by accident. My manoeuvres come out by training and consistent practice." **– Daida**

Left: Popular spots can be crowded. Best to check your landing zone!

Opposite: Kevin Pritchard goes high. Even on flat water freestyle has no limits.

360

For a carving 360, you want to be nicely powered up but not over-powered. If the sail is really tugging, you'll be forced into a long shallow turn whereas the only way to complete a smooth 360 is to initiate steeply and carve a much tighter arc than for a standard gybe. Half way through, at the time you'd normally flip the rig, oversheet, draw it back over the tail and lay it right down. As it backwinds, drop your shoulders over the boom to stop it blasting you backwards and keep the carve going. As the turn unwinds and you drop off the plane, place the front foot up by the mastfoot to keep the board level. Head to wind, let the rig blow upright, sheet in, bear away and complete the revolution.

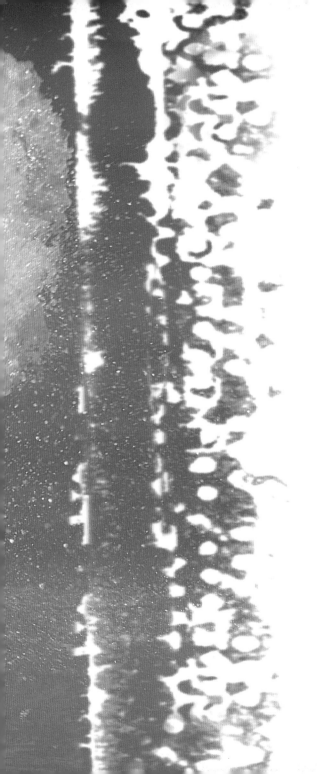

7
crystal ball
– the future of windsurfing

"Windsurfing is my life right now. I travel all around the world and sail and train for the competitions. Since I started to compete professionally, my life has not been the same. Now I don't spend so much time at home and I spend a lot of time travelling and competing around the world. It is really fun and I will keep doing it for as long as I am able. Most people sit in the office working in front of computers all week and only get the chance to practise their sport on the weekends. I get to practise my sport every day and my sponsors support me. I cannot ask for more. Sometimes it's not easy to stay away for a long time, and we also have a lot of responsibilities and projects to do, like reports, testing, modelling, promotional trips and interviews." – **Daida**

Windsurfing has progressed at an inconceivable pace in the last twenty years. Equipment has evolved so far that it's hard to believe the original 4 metre, 20kg Windsurfer and today's 4kg 'cocktail sticks' are part of the same sport.

At the Weymouth Speed Trials in 1980, an early windsurfer clocked 20 knots – an extraordinary speed for the time. Today the record stands at over 45.5 knots, more than 50mph. Only one highly specialised uni-directional yacht has been faster and that disintegrated at the end of its record breaking run. When the weathermen predict gales, structural damage and tell us

to stay indoors, windsurfers rejoice. In 50 knots of wind, Storm Force 10, windsurfers are the ONLY pleasure craft on the water; but more than that, they're actually in control and enjoying the conditions.

Some say, and they're right, that windsurfing begins when you're planing and that once you've planed, you're hooked for life. In the beginning it took maybe two or three years of battling to break through the Force 4 barrier. Today anyone with the time to practise can be hooked in the harness and planing within a couple of months of their first go. What's more, there's equipment available now that planes in 6 knots of wind – that's barely a zephyr. That planing buzz is now more accessible than ever.

So what happens now? Windsurfing lost itself for a while as the major companies tried to 'out tech' each other. But the design brief has turned around. Now the race is to make things as simple as

Above: The sky's the limit.

Opposite: Push yourself! – Daida

"windsurfers are now **pushing** the **limits** to a **life threatening** degree"

possible. We haven't got time in our busy lives to spend hours rigging and 'tweaking'. We want to throw it all together in seconds and get out there but still get top performance. If it's a hassle people will go for the instant gratification of a jet ski.

We're unlikely to see radical design changes (how many times have the prophets said that?) so much as a gradual refinement. Ever more exotic laminates and moulding processes will allow us to get board weights down to 4kg or less AND make them bullet proof. The same goes for rigs. Super light carbon masts and booms and a billion hours experimentation with sail twist and foil shape, have left us with standard rotational rigs which are faster than the pro race rigs of five years ago but which are half the weight and ten times easier to handle. As rigs and boards get lighter, the less energy is needed to make them perform so the window for yet more spectacular tricks gets ever wider.

In terms of human performance, the standard of wave sailing has risen more in the last year than at any other time and the feeling is that it's only just beginning. Perhaps looking to emulate the same wild spirit of the extreme skiers and snowboarders, windsurfers are now pushing the limits to a life threatening degree. Double forwards are now commonplace so how long will it be before we see the first triple? The double back loop has yet to be spotted in competition – that won't be long coming. The table top forward was one of the first and most radical combination jumps but what others might we see? Perhaps a push loop followed by a forward or a forward integrated into a Vulcan? As for wave riding ... well when they first rode Jaws, they were happy to drop straight down the wave and head directly for the safety of the channel. Now they ride it like a normal wave, bottom turning at 40mph and then climbing 30 foot back up to smack that enormous lip. There's easily enough room inside that vast tube for a windsurfer and his rig. And who says Jaws is the biggest windsurfable wave? Extremists like Laird Hamilton travel the world in search of outer reefs, which on the right day may provide the ride of a lifetime.

One area where the surface has barely been scratched is Freestyle. One day we will look back and laugh at the pathetic simplicity of the tricks being performed

Opposite: Wave sailing has moved on at a rapid pace.

Above: Windsurfing is a perfect vehicle for self-expression.

Below: With so many beautiful places to sail, there is always a good reason to go windsurfing.

now. Freestyle boards have a long way to go. Like wakeboards, some will become more 'twin tipped' with small fins in the nose to give them more control going backwards. Taking away the complication of the elements, gymnastically the current tricks are relatively straightforward. But when, like the aerial skiers, the specialist windsurfing freestylers start training on trampolines and in swimming pools, then we could see the jumps and transitions take on a new complexity.

There has always been a large cross over between windsurfing and other board sports. The simplifying and concentration of technology in equipment could bring other boardriders into the sport. There are now clear parallels between surfing and wave riding, snowboarding, skateboarding and freestyle. Windsurfing will always survive and thrive because it has so much to offer everyone from the image conscious adolescent to the ambitious pensioner.

Windsurfing as a sport will entertain, thrill, amaze and scare you. But it will always be fun and that remains the most important thing. So, if you've found yourself gazing out to see if it's windy, don't resist any longer – get out there!

"I'll still be windsurfing in twenty years time, with a family and such, and possibly involved in windsurfing, maybe helping others involved in it." – **Nik**

"I hope we see more and more sailors every year. It will probably be an easier sport in the future, because we will have better, more refined equipment, and this will make it so much more accessible to more people." – **Daida**

Opposite: Competition has intensified with major equipment developments.

Above & Right: Aerials are higher, faster and keep on improving.

8
glossary

Break: Term derived from surfing to describe the waves and where they start breaking.

Carve: To alter your course at high speed by jamming on the rail and banking the board.

Cavitation: This occurs when air collects around the fin causing it to lose its grip in the water – also known as spin out.

Cheese Roll: A lateral aerial forward roll named after its inventor, Cesare Cantagalli.

Chill factor: Getting cold from the wind lowering your body temperature, also know as wind chill.

Crosshore: When the wind blows across the beach running parallel with the waves.

Downhaul: The rope used to apply tension to the luff of the sail. Crank it on!

Downwind: Sailing with the wind behind you.

Eye of the wind: Precise direction from which the wind is coming.

Footstraps: Straps to put your feet into keep connected to the board.

Freestyle: Performing tricks on the board for a panel of judges or just for fun.

Gybing: Changing course so that the stern passes through the eye of the wind.

Harness: A device that takes the strain from a sailor's arms and back, for energy efficiency.

Hypothermia: A dangerous drop in body core temperature caused by prolonged exposure to the elements.

Jaws: One of the largest waves in the world that breaks on the north shore of Maui, Hawaii and is sailed only by the world's best and most daring windsurfers.

Leech: The back, or trailing edge of the sail.

Lip: The crest of the wave when it has just started to break.

Luffing: Heading up towards the wind. Also describes the act of the sail flapping.

Mast foot: The assembly at the base of the mast that connects the rig to the board.

Offshore wind: A wind blowing from the land out to sea.

Onshore wind: A wind blowing off the sea towards the land.

Peak: The point where the wave breaks first.

Peel: The act of the wave breaking evenly in one direction.

Pintail: A board with a tapering stern for better control.

Plane: When the board is skimming along on top of the water, rather than displacing it.

Point up: Sailing the board closer to the wind.

Port: Left, looking forward.

PWA: Professional Windsurfers Association.

Rail: The edge of the board from tail to nose.

Rig: Combination of mast, sail, boom and mast foot.

Rocker: Curvature of the board running from fore to aft.

Rocket air: Hit the lip, sheet in and head for the stars!

Sheet: (in/out) Nautical term for rope adopted by windsurfers. Sheeting in or out refers to pulling the rope in or letting it out on a dinghy or yacht to increase or decrease the power in the sail.

Shove it: Kicking the tail of the board out behind you and laying down the sail before recovering and sailing on.

Sideshore: See crosshore.

Sinker: A board that will not support the dead weight of the sailor and rig when not in motion.

Spin Out: See 'cavitation'.

Spock: Freestyle move where the board is spun through 360 on its nose named by sailors for reasons known only to them! Variations include one handed and 540.

Starboard: Right, looking forward.

Stern: Back end of the board.

Tack: A turn where the nose of the board passes through the eye of the wind.

Tack upwind: Sail a zigzag course to make ground against the wind.

Universal joint: The invention upon which the whole concept of windsurfing is based. The joint that connects the rig to the board and allows the mast to be tilted in any way through 360 degrees.

Uphaul: Rope attached to the end of the boom and the mastfoot. Used to raise the sail from the water in the days before waterstarts!

Upwind: Sailing with the wind on your forward facing shoulder.

Vulcan: Freestyle move where the board is turned through 180 degrees on its nose, continuing the Star Trek theme, see Spock.

Waterstart: Starting in the water and allowing the sail to help lift you onto the board avoiding the need to use the uphaul.

Willy Skipper: Freestyle move. Jumping the board round 180 degrees and continuing to sail the board standing on the nose. One can only guess where the name comes from!

Windward: The windward side of the board is the side of the board the wind hits first.

Wipe-out: To take a fall as a result of pilot error.

360: Spinning through 360 degrees and continuing in the same direction. Can be performed on flat water, on the face of a wave or mid air!

Chilli is the global agency specialising in Freesports such as windsurfing.

Chilli provides services and products which include strategic consultancy, campaign implementation, event and TV production, media exploitation and design.

To find out more about the range of Freesports video titles available from Chilli visit chillivideo.com

For more information on Chilli please contact: info@chilli-news.com

Other titles available in this series:

The Ultimate Guide to Mountain biking
The Ultimate Guide to Surfing

Forthcoming titles from Chilli and HarperCollins*Publishers*:

The Ultimate Guide to Snowboarding
The Ultimate Guide to Skateboarding
The Ultimate Guide to In-line Skating